{ *for married people* }

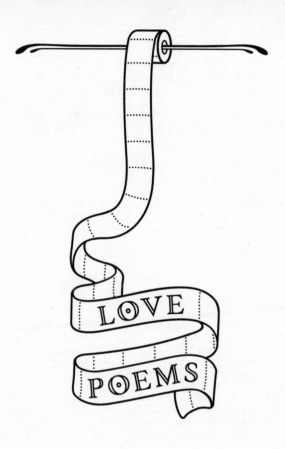

LOVE

POEMS

{ *for married people* }

JOHN KENNEY

BANTAM PRESS

TRANSWORLD PUBLISHERS
61–63 Uxbridge Road, London W5 5SA
www.penguin.co.uk

Transworld is part of the Penguin Random House group of companies
whose addresses can be found at global.penguinrandomhouse.com

First published in the United States of America in 2018 by G. P. Putnam's Sons
an imprint of Penguin Publishing Group
a division of Penguin Random House LLC

First published in Great Britain in 2019 by Bantam Press
an imprint of Transworld Publishers
Published by arrangement with G. P. Putnam's Sons

A CIP catalogue record for this book
is available from the British Library.

ISBN 9781787631731

Typeset in 12.3/17.1 pt Granjon LT Std by Jouve (UK), Milton Keynes
Printed and bound in Great Britain by Clays Ltd, Elcograf S.p.A.

Penguin Random House is committed to a sustainable future
for our business, our readers and our planet. This book is made
from Forest Stewardship Council® certified paper.

1 3 5 7 9 10 8 6 4 2

For ~~Barbara~~
~~Karen~~
~~Pam~~
~~Miss France~~
~~Claudine~~
~~Ramone~~
Lissa

All poets write bad poetry.
Bad poets publish them, good poets burn them.

—UMBERTO ECO

{ *for married people* }

**I honor you and our love but I also lost track of time
at a bar with my coworkers**

In France, *cinq à sept* was once sacrosanct,
a euphemism for rendezvous,
for the thing that men and women do.

But we are not in France.
We are here, in Montclair, New Jersey.
And it is well past seven.
And I promised to be home at six.

And, yes, that's booze on my breath.
The guys and I had one . . . fine, three drinks after work.

And apparently I have forgotten the milk.
And the bread and the pasta and the pull-ups.
And the allergy medicine.

Why are you dressed up?
Wait. Today is Valentine's Day?

Are you in the mood?

I am.
Let's put the kids down.
Have a light dinner.
Shower.
Maybe not drink so much.
And do that thing I would rather do with you than
    anyone else.
Lie in bed and look at our iPhones.

Our love

Our love is like the padlocks on the Pont des Arts, in
     Paris.
Thousands of locks, symbols of unbreakable love.
Isn't that beautiful?

Apparently, though, all those locks are
too heavy for the bridge.
Did you hear this?
I read it somewhere.

The locks are weighing the bridge down.
So you know what they're going to do?
They're taking them off with bolt cutters and throwing
     them in the trash.
Isn't that beautiful, too?

So now the people aren't locked together anymore.
They're free to maybe see other people.
I thought that was interesting.

Why are you in the shower with me?

Did the bathtub shrink?
I ask because here we are,
naked,
showering together,
like we once did all the time.
Remember? At the beginning?
We would stand and talk,
seals slipping by one another,
a playful ease letting the other into the stream.
Now?
I'm not sure what you're doing in here.
I'm freezing.
There's shampoo stinging my eyes.
You just stepped on my foot.
For the love of Christ who flushed the toilet?
Because I'm being scalded alive.
Get out.
Now.
It was a nice idea though, honey.
Could you close the door?

Is it possible you are sending me a sexy signal?

The kids are finally down
and you are looking
at me in that way.
Tease.

Or are you
just spacing out?
Wait.
Yup,
you're spacing out.

You unzip your skirt
and your baggy underpants
ride way, way up on your hips.
How old are those, anyway?

You pull on some sweatpants
and a T-shirt and a sweater and a fleece
and I am not able to
make out any contour of your body at all.

I think you are sending me
a signal in the way that
married couples
send each other signals.

And just so we're clear
you're signaling
I'm going to call my sister and order sushi.
You should do something, too.

You are different

I want to share my life with you.
I do.
I said those words
in front of all our friends.
As well as your incredibly annoying family.
You're different.
That's what I thought
when we met.
I told my friends.
He's different.
(They said you weren't.)
And now we are married
for life.
Is that right?
(Wow! That seems really long now!)
But here's something.
You're different
from, like, when we met.
Your OkCupid profile said

I like running and hiking and cooking!

Have you ever cooked?

And you seem to have parked that running thing for a
    while.

I'm kind of thinking a lot of that was

bullshit.

If we were to redo your profile

hypothetically

what would we write?

I like sitting.

Not showering.

I enjoy putting my hand down the front of my shorts and
    scratching my balls.

And occasionally looking up at my new wife

and saying what's up.

Which is a weird thing to say to your wife.

Yogurt

You went to Trader Joe's.
And took the kids.
So I could do a work call.

You bought the week's shopping.
And my call was canceled.
So I scrolled around YouTube.

I don't really know where the three hours went.
Though maybe I napped?

I'll tell you what I didn't do.
I didn't unload the dishwasher
like you asked.

Or switch the laundry.
Or call the plumber.
Or that other thing you asked that I forgot.

And now, watching you put away the groceries
surveying all you've done for us today
I feel the need to thank you.

Well, more a question than a thanks.
And granted the tone of it isn't great.
And from your expression I know now I'm fucked.
But seriously, how did you forget the yogurt?

When are you planning to turn off your Kindle?

They say love is light.
I think they do.
I'm not really sure.
I might have heard that in a Subaru commercial.
The point is that I see your light right now.
And I wish I didn't.
Because I'm really tired.
And I had a long day.
And I have to get up early tomorrow.
All of which you know.

Another thing they say is that a man can know a thing
    but forget it almost instantly.
Like a goldfish.
I sigh the sigh I sigh when I'm annoyed.
But you don't hear me.
Because you have earbuds in.
And are watching what appears to be a video of people
    body-surfing on pudding.

And here I thought you were reading a book.

Maybe love is like light.
In that it can dim, fade, go out completely.
Seriously. Would it kill you to watch that in the
    bathroom?

Date night

Who are you . . .

What?

. . . texting. I was just wondering . . .

Sorry. What?

You're texting and I just . . .

Client. Sorry. Wait. They're changing a . . .

What?

Meeting. Tomorrow now.

Oh. Okay. Well. I guess I'll check . . .

Done. So. Who are you . . .

One second. Sorry. Fuck.

Work?

What?

Is it work?

Wait. I told them where the file was.

Who?

What?

Nothing.

Dammit. It's on the thumb drive. They know that . . .

What is?
What?
Nothing.
This restaurant is nice.
What?

Bedtime

Now we are in the bedroom in our underpants.
Let's turn the lights down.
No, further.
Off, I guess, is the technical term.
Maybe try a towel under the door
where that sliver of light is coming in.
What if we cuddle?
And by cuddle I mean not actually touch.
Each of us at the far edge
of our own side
of the bed.
Why does this feel like a twin bed?
You're so close.
I have a fun sexy idea.
Let's close our eyes
and see who can keep them closed the longest.
For the next, like, seven hours or so.
I like you.

I breathe you

I am dreaming
but it feels so real.

A man. Is it you?
Not even close.

It's Rob, Casey's husband.
The one with the Italian accent.

We are on a beach.
Rob and me, not you.

He chases me
playfully. And we laugh.

Then my tops falls off.
Oops, I giggle.
And he catches me.

And then, a terrible smell.
Like garbage. Wet dog. Death.

I am blinking and awake
your breath hot on my face.

You son of a bitch.
Rob, come back.

Orgy

Autumn
overcast and cool
woodsmoke-scented air
leaves in the yard.

We decided to go out back
among the tall hedgerows to
rake and bag the leaves.

You said in a very sexy voice
We're out of garbage bags.
And in your shrugging I might have seen
your breasts move

had they not been covered under
your fleece
sweatshirt
and work shirt.

Well. I'm going in, you said after a while.
Later, we heated up Dinty Moore beef stew
and then you went to bed.
I watched half of a Jason Bourne movie.

Did I say orgy?
Sorry, my mind wandered.
I meant yard work.

Bathroom door

Super minor point.
Not a big deal at all.
But I think I missed
the family meeting
where we decided
it was a good idea
to keep the bathroom door
open
while you are urinating
smiling and waving
saying *hey hon*
and trying to talk to me
when I pass by.
See
what happens to me
is that the magic dies a little.
I die a little.

At the kitchen sink

I was feeling
fondness
for you

As you gave me
a shoulder massage
at the sink.

What a small
lovely surprise.

And then you
cupped my boobs
and made a *wha-wha* noise.

And in an instant
I felt disgust
and sadness and regret.

The fertility process

If you had told me
when I was sixteen
that a beautiful woman would demand sex from me
    every day
I would have said impossible.
But here we are
having rushed home from work.
On the clock.
Egg dropped.
Sweet, sweet lovemaking.
But also not unlike a class at Equinox that you have to
    pre–sign up for.
You whisper sweet nothings to me.
I really hope you haven't been masturbating
because the doctor said you need to build up sperm.
Oh.
Okay.
Well, I have some bad news on that front.

Let's spice things up

That's what you said
when we were ordering
in the Mexican restaurant.
And I said
Ohmigod
are you serious?
And you smiled
and said *totally.*
Spicey is nicey you said
in a weird accent
laughing
but also a little embarrassed at the weird accent thing.
And I said
it would have to be with a woman though
not a guy.
And you said
What are you talking about?
And I said

aren't you talking about

having a threesome?

You get a look on your face sometimes.

And you got it here.

And you said

I was talking about getting the mole and maybe some
*   pico de gallo.*

To which I said

Oh.

Okay.

That's a good idea, too.

I cry as you drive away

Standing on the sidewalk
alone
I wave
as the car pulls away.
You, the kids, the dog.

Bye! I say.
Bye, guys!

A long weekend at your mother's upstate.
What fun.
But Dad has work to do.

Well, not a lot of work.
It shouldn't take more than a few hours actually.
And truth be told it's not due for two weeks.
I certainly could have gone.
Shoot.

But now you've driven away.
And I am here.
Alone.
At home.
In the quiet.
Without pants.
And there's so much beer.
That's why I'm crying
as you drive away.

Is this the right time for that?

Standing at the door
ready to go
tapping my foot.
(We are late to my sister's surprise party)
I turn and see you
standing in the kitchen
like a man on a summer afternoon by a lake
casually adjusting a fishing pole.
Only it's not a fishing pole.
It's fingernail clippers.
And you are cutting your fingernails
over the sink.
You look up and perhaps because of the expression on my
    face
you say, *what?*
It would be impossible for me to explain
if you don't already understand.

Corduroys

Just the other day
you said to me
accusatorily
Well, I guess I don't have any corduroys *anymore.*

One, I did not throw out your pants.
Two, I have never seen you wear corduroys.
Three, it's June.

Sexting isn't this, apparently

I did not know
during the monthly rote calisthenics of our sex
that you would be upset
if I sent a quick text message to my college roommate Marie

> who texted back and asked if I'd watched *The Crown*.
> I texted *yes!!! It's amazing.*
> *I love*
> *Claire Foy.*

And I guess I was surprised
and from the look on your face
you were certainly surprised
that I was sexting.

> Except you said
> that's not sexting.
> So I texted Marie to ask her and she texted back
> *LOL!!! Are you really having sex right now?*

I said I was but not anymore.
You had stormed out of the room and
tripped and
fell in the hall.

And Marie said
That's a little funny.
I sent a smiley emoji
because it was a little funny.

Emily's name isn't Rachel

You remember so much that isn't useful.
World War II battles and
facts about the Constitutional Congress.
The Red Sox lineup from 2004 and
dialogue from the movie *Butch Cassidy and the Sundance Kid*.
But on the way to the neighbor's party
you ask the question you always ask.
The one you've asked a hundred times. A thousand?
What's Gary's wife's name? Is it Rachel?
Nope. It's not Rachel. It's never been Rachel. It's Emily.
And she's from Boston, you say.
No. What? No. She's from Los Angeles.
Huh. Who's from Boston? Her ex-husband Greg?
No ex-husband. No one named Greg. Gary. Just . . . Gary.
I thought Rachel had family in the Boston area.
What are you talking about?
And their kids are Peter and Grace, right?
Not even close. Astrid and Colette.
Weird. I could have sworn . . .

You have the address? I ask.

Oh sure. 248 Sycamore Lane.

9 Oriole Street, I say.

Really? Who the heck am I thinking of then?

No idea. Just please tell me you remembered the beer and
   wine.

. . . Absolutely.

On waking late and realizing that I hit on your best friend at your birthday party

My head hurts
and I am still fully clothed.
I guess sorry is in order.
But I would kill for a coffee first.
Honey?
Hello?
Why are my clothes on the lawn?

Couples counseling (part 1)

The couples therapist urges
us to repeat
what each of us
has just said.

Okay. So I hear you saying
that I am a terrible husband,
man, and human being.

Hold on, Roger, the therapist says.
That's not what Amy said.
Yes, but that's what I heard.
*Okay but what she actually said was she wanted you to listen
    more.*
Let's try to repeat the actual words
and not our interpretation.

Sorry, I wasn't listening . . .

But I don't say that part out loud.
Unfortunately, what I do say is,
Do you have Wi-Fi here?

Who were you thinking about?

You.

Of course you.

Who else would I have been thinking about?

My coworker Alex, who always seems tan?

Or Carlos from SoulCycle?

Please.

Our love is deeper than that, Craig.

I mean Daryl.

I know your name is Daryl.

But right then I was thinking of Craig from Starbucks
    who has those blue eyes.

But you are my husband and we are married for life.

And yes I think of you during these intimate moments.

By that I mean you certainly cross my mind.

You're in there.

In the mix.

You would be in the credits if it were a movie.

Way down though.

Guy in sweater.
Just . . . shhh.
Don't worry about it.

What time should we leave for the airport?

I have a car service coming at 7.

But isn't our flight at 9:30?

Yes. Why?

Seven. Wow. Okay. So 7:00 is cutting it close, don't you
    think?

For a 9:30 flight?

Fine. Whatever. Do what you want.

Don't be like that. I'll do 6:45.

Sure.

Seriously? That's not early enough?

If it were me I would do 6:15. Maybe even 6:00. The 405 is
    a nightmare.

But we've already checked in. And we have no bags to
    check.

Ahh, hello? Security lines?

Why are you talking like that?

Whatever.

I'm calling now. I'm making it for 6:00.

Five forty-five might be smarter.

You've got to be kidding me.

I don't kid about traffic.

Did you take something?

Look. All I'm saying is that if it were me, I'd do 5:30. I would make it for 5:30.

Why not 5:00?

I don't know if that's your sarcastic voice but I agree a hundred percent.

Okay then. I am now calling and making a reservation for a car at 5:00 A.M. tomorrow.

A.M.? Isn't the flight in the evening?

We finish each other's . . .

You guys, it was the worst hotel ever
you said.
You were telling the story
at the dinner party
about the horrible vacation.
The rooms . . .
Smelled of cigarette smoke, I said, jumping in
because I think I tell it better.
But you kept going.
Shh, David. Cigarette smoke. And we asked . . .
We asked to switch rooms! Three times! I said. But . . .
All the rooms smelled the same. David!
Like smoke, I added, needlessly,
looking at you, because I was telling it.
Even though you were telling it first.
But I think we can agree that seriously
I tell it better.
But I get the sense that you don't agree.
Because you looked at me and said in your quiet angry
    voice,

I'm telling it.

And you said *So we ask this adorable little man at the front desk . . .*

No no. Before that we see a guy smoking . . .

We saw him after we went to the front desk . . .

No. Before. And we ask the guy, Do you have any non-smoking rooms.

And he says . . .

Oh yes, you can smoke in any of them!

You are such an asshole sometimes, you said.

It got quiet after that.

And then I said, the concierge didn't say the asshole part to us, just the smoke thing.

We haven't been invited to a dinner party in a while have we?

Seafood?

I meant to tell you
as I was driving home from
the mall earlier
I heard that marvelous song by Beyoncé.

I forget the name
but she sings
about things
that I liked a lot.

One in particular
was this.
When he fuck me good
I take his ass to Red Lobster.

Isn't that interesting?
And the funny thing is
Shrimp Fest
is going on right now.

I would be happy to take your behind (ha ha!)
to the restaurant of your choice
were you to uphold
your part of the deal.

No?
Very good.
We could also just do chicken.

Couples counseling (part 2)

I acknowledge that
I shouldn't have asked about Wi-Fi.
And I acknowledge that I wasn't
listening to or respecting Amy.
I would also like to acknowledge
that I hate the word "acknowledge."

This is what I'm talking about
Amy says to the therapist,
who then asks Amy to acknowledge her feelings
by speaking directly to Roger.
Fine. Roger, I'm hearing from the tone
of your voice
that you are exasperated and don't mean your
    acknowledgment.
I don't, I say
out loud
which is a surprise
as I thought I was only thinking it.

Dickhead, you say.

Amy, the therapist says. *His name is Roger.*

Really? Amy asks.

Because he looks to me like a dickhead.

What I meant to say to your mother when she called and you were out with friends

Your daughter is out with friends
and I am here alone with the kids, I said.
How nice, she said.
How are my grandkids?
How are you, Steve?
Me? I'm fine. Fine.
Your voice sounds a little strange, she said.
Oh, you know.
Life and work and stress and the kids.
It's fine.
But I do find a kind of deep sadness
overwhelms me most days.
I think that's pretty common though.
Do you ever feel like you're dying?
Ever look at a fork and have no idea of the name of it?
No? Oh.
What? Yes, that's a cork being opened, why?
I guess it's just that

of *course* the wheels
on the bus go round and round.
What else would they do?
And this fucking wipers situation.
If they go swish, swish, swish
you *have* to replace them.
I mean Jesus *Christ!*
What I meant to say was
Hey, Fran, how are you?

You reach for me in the middle of the night

You wake
moaning in the dark.
A dirty dream?
Or your head cold?
Either way
you reach for
my body.
Well hello there, I say,
reaching over for you.
Though you are still feeling around
like you've lost a contact lens
and not for my penis.
Still, a rare middle-of-the-night
interlude.
Care to be rude?

But as I caress you
you sit up
fully waking.

I need it, you say.
Then I'm your man, I say.

What are you doing? you ask.
I need a Kleenex.
My nose is running.
Go back to sleep.

Let's talk about my underpants

La Perla.
Victoria's Secret.
Calvin Klein.
If you want skimpy, sexy lingerie
you should buy some.
And then wear them yourself.

You dog-ear the catalogues for me.
Hot, you write.
How sweet.
Do I ask you about your
Less-than-Bradley-Cooper-like boxers?
No. But I could.

Do you know who makes a great line?
Walmart.
It's called "Big Unders."
I like that name.
They're white, come five to a pack.

One size fits all, it says.

You could use them as a parachute.

Or a hammock.

Or to cover your middle-aged bum.

I like to put them on in front of you and watch your face.

But . . . but . . . those look like an Indian dhoti, you say,
    confused.

I know, I say, smiling.

And they're machine washable.

Now that's my idea of sexy.

While failing to correctly assemble an IKEA cabinet, I consider my manhood

When I say out loud
What the fuck is this piece for
I'm not asking you a question.
I'm saying what the fuck is this piece for.
And yes, I am fully aware that what I've made so far
does not look like the picture on the box.
What's that? you say.
Oh. I see. Maybe the whole thing is upside down.
Shit.
No, we're not going to call "a guy."
I'm a guy.
I can build things.
Not like your father, who built a cabin by himself.
Or your old boyfriend, mister wonderful
the contractor.
Nor can I grow a big beard
like him
because I have the face of a small boy

with random patches of kitten-like hair.
And no, I didn't know that a hex key and an Allen
     wrench
were essentially the same thing.
And I have never used a power saw.
And am bizarrely afraid of water bugs.
But I am a man in the strictest biological sense
if not the ideal Special Forces candidate.
Big deal, I'm crying.
Here. You do it.

Couples counseling (part 3)

Let's try some
role play
the therapist says.
Roger
you start.
And Roger
let's remember that
role play
isn't where
you pretend
Amy
is her friend
Jennifer.

We will be different

When we have
children,
they will watch almost no
television.

Painting and drawing and music,
this will be their
muse.

Board games and cards.
What fun they will have.
Us too.

Fast forward
seven years
and it is 6 A.M.
on a Sunday morning
and Mommy and Daddy
had too much to drink at the party.

Do you know who our muse is now?
That's right
SpongeBob.
One after another
after another.

You're damn right
you can have Mentos
for breakfast, kids.

I ask my coworker, Tim, who doesn't have children, how his weekend was

A-ma-zing, he says, eyes wide.
It was amazing.
Just me and Michael.
We slept in
got coffee at that new place
in the Village.
Have you been? No?
Then we strolled through Central Park.
Wandered over to the Goya show at the Met.
Incredible.
Have you seen it? No?
Rode Citi Bikes to Coney Island.
Had pizza at Di Fara's.
You've eaten there right? No?
I thought you lived in Brooklyn.
Huh.
Went for a swim.
Found a great ice cream place.

Took the train back to our place and had sex.

Took a nap.

Isn't that the best part of the weekend?

Sex and naps?

You have a weird expression.

Then on a whim we

bought scalper tickets for *Hamilton*.

Have you seen it? No? Really? Wow.

This was our third time.

Later we found this amazing jazz club and stayed till
four.

We walked over the Fifty-Ninth Street Bridge and
watched the sun come up.

Then we went home and slept till noon.

How was your weekend?

Well, Tim, we went to a kid's birthday party at
Chuck E. Cheese

And made inane small talk

with other parents we have nothing in common with.

Have you been? No? Amazing.

What's the plan for dinner?

Like swallows to Capistrano
you call me each afternoon from work.
Quick point on the swallows thing.
I'm not saying swallows call.
I guess I just mean they perform, on schedule,
the same damned ritual.

Hey. What's up? you say, distracted,
reading an email.
What's the plan for dinner?
I don't know, I say
looking at a purse on the Fossil site.
I'm at work. Like you.
Chicken? you ask
toggling over to the Body Issue of espn.com.

Sure, I say, already having forgotten what we're talking
about.

Can you get ice cream? you ask
clicking over to huffpo.
So I'm getting dinner then, I say
enhancing a picture of Ryan Reynolds.
I can get it, you say, drained of energy
as if you've just received news of a death.

We have leftover pasta, I say
picturing Ryan Reynolds naked in a Four Seasons hotel
    room.
I hate leftovers, you say, swallow-like, so predictable.
I bet Ryan Reynolds isn't predictable.
Except I say that last part out loud.

Our love is tested in traffic

What would Jesus do
in this bumper-to-bumper mess on the BQE
going four miles an hour?
I'll tell you what he probably wouldn't do.
He wouldn't call the old woman in the Ford Focus
with the handicapped plates
who slipped in ahead of us
a cocksucker.
Because that's not nice. And probably not true.

How exactly am I not supporting you right now?
Fine, we'll never go to the beach again.
Okay, we should have left earlier.
Yes, the kids will get to bed late and that ruins your life.
I know, the wine store will be closed by the time we get
        home.

Wow, that was a string of astounding obscenities.
You know the kids are in the back seat, right?

Is now the wrong time to ask
how that Buddhist meditation app
you raved about
is working out for you?

Would it be possible to stop volunteering me for things?

Earlier
at the school carnival
a parent whose name I don't know said
Your wife said you were doing the bounce house!
That's the worst ha ha!
I didn't know that I was doing the bounce house.
Or that it was the worst.
I assumed the cotton candy machine
was the worst.
That's what you volunteered me for
last year.

It was ninety degrees and humid and no shade.
Other parents waving and smiling.
Or were they laughing at me?
I think they were.
But I was badly dehydrated
covered with spun sugar.

Kids crying.
That doesn't look like cotton candy
one angry mother said.
Go die, I wanted to say
But didn't.
Though maybe my expression did?

And now
late in the afternoon
Not a cold beer in sight
my sweaty, sticky forced-smile face
wedged through
a hole in a piece of plywood
painted to look like a barnyard.
And I am a fat pig
wearing a stovepipe hat.
The kids are laughing now
because they are throwing pies in my face.
And it kind of hurts.
Ha ha! Look at Paul
you say, laughing.
Your face clean and pie free
He loves to volunteer.
No, he doesn't.
Paul hates this shit.

Couples counseling (part 4)

The therapist gave us homework.
Make a list, she said.
Of the things you love
about each other.
You slurp soup.
That sucking sound
is killing me.
You say that burping after a meal in China is a
show of respect for the cook.
I think that's bullshit.
Also we live in Chicago.
You can't teach an old dog new tricks
you say, laughing.
Perhaps.
But you can put an old dog down and kill it.

What's that? you ask.
Oh nothing, honey.
How's your list?

Ode to your psychopharmacologist

Dear doctor pill man
who doles out love in milligrams.
Alchemist.
Magic mix.
Mixologist.
Husband: behaved.
Marriage: saved.
I would not be around
had we not found
that perfect combo
of Zoloft and Lexapro.
You're a pro.
I thank you so.

Upon reflection, I wish we had left my company holiday party a little earlier

We rode the elevator down with my boss.
My new boss at the new job I really like.
You, my husband, drunk.
     Him, not so much.
You stood so close to him
your back to the elevator door.
He looked uncomfortable.
I cringed.
   Lovely party, he said to you
     trying to pull himself back into the elevator wall.
   You're a lovely party, you said.
     Which made no sense.
Then you hugged him
and put your head on his shoulder.
   And he said, *Oh my*
     while you sang, softly sang,
       When a man loves a woman.

So there's that.

(Editor's note: a haiku is a Japanese poem of seventeen syllables, in three lines of five, seven, and five, traditionally evoking images of the natural world.)

Why a haiku Stu?
Because my divorce lawyer
Found your girlfriend's text

. . .

I'll call nine-one-one
Because your penis is stuck
In your zipper hon

. . .

Pam's got quite a rack
Is not what I want to hear
When you meet my friends

. . .

To my new in-laws
You keep stopping by, no call
I won't open door.

Mother's Day

I didn't know who Marie Kondo was.
Author of the international best-seller
The Life-Changing Magic of Tidying Up.
What a funny, funny
Mother's Day gift that was.
How we should fold clothes with "love."
How we should only keep things that "spark joy."
You know what doesn't spark joy
for me a lot of times?
You.
Should I keep you?
And the card was a thoughtful touch.
"You know what you are?"
It asked on the wacky cover.
"A mother!"
And you signed it
Your husband, Russell.
That certainly sparked something for me.

Thoughts on the expression on your face while
I explain the discomfort of my recent prostate exam

Honey
you have no idea
how uncomfortable it is
having a man's finger up your ass.
Though your face suggests
that you are unimpressed.

You have no idea what pain like that feels like,
I say, pouring a large gin.
I mean, he's pressing against my prostate.

You nod.
Arms folded.
How could I? you ask.
Natural childbirth.
No drugs.
No epidural.
Nine pounds five ounces.
How big was the doctor's finger again?

You sort of thought of me

Thank you for thinking of me
sort of
on my birthday.
You asked me what I wanted
and I said oh nothing.
But you asked again
and I said jewelry might be nice.
Earrings maybe.
Diamond ones
you said with a sly smile.
And I smiled too.
And then it was my birthday
and you gave me a gift card to
Banana Republic.
I think they have jewelry there
you said.
They sure do. But
not diamonds.
Thank you.

My vasectomy

yes, we have four children
and I promised we wouldn't have more
after the third

that said, i don't know why
you have to be here
in person, in the surgical room

and no, honey, the doctor
is not going to let you make
the snip

oh wait
he is
honey honey honey

to which you laugh
and say

it wasn't a good idea to
get pregnant at forty with our fourth child, either.

you have a weird look on your face,
honey?
careful.

I don't think it is remotely funny
that your father jokingly questions
my sexual orientation

No, I did not go to la-di-da university.
I went to Yale.
And your father is well aware of that.
Why would he say that?
And why does he call me
Lady Mary
just because I like *Downton Abbey*?
I know he's old
and set in his ways
and was in the Marine Corps
and thinks the squirrels in his yard are communists.
But honest to God
he has to stop referring to me as
Swishy McJackass.
And no
I should not have told him

that I was once
a Cub Scout.
That was a mistake
that I regret every time I see him.

To Lissa. No kidding.

You called me
and said you were meeting friends
for beers at a bar that had bocce.

I was surprised.
We knew each other
though not well.
But Sunday evening
in late fall we drank beer
and talked like old friends.

Your friends never showed.
Were they ever coming?
It got late and we left.
Standing on the corner,
it didn't feel like just meeting for a beer anymore.

I hadn't wanted to leave my apartment that evening.
Because it was easier to stay in.
It was easier to be alone.

Except you ruined my sad little life.
You kissed me.

How strange that it happens like that.
If we had just parted at the corner.
A whole life never lived.

I proposed in Paris
at a café across from a fountain
by an old church.

I guess I just wanted to say
thank you.
For saving my life.
For helping me un-become the person I was.
For staying when it would have been easier to leave.

For Lulu and Hewitt.

We passed a guy on a bench once.
He was playing a kazoo
partially dressed like a clown
and wore ski goggles.
It was summer.

That would have been you, you said, smiling.
If you hadn't met me.

And it's probably true.
It's certainly true that you
could have done better.
But I most assuredly could not.

I just hope it doesn't take a poet
for you to know that.

ACKNOWLEDGMENTS

This book was not my idea. If you haven't enjoyed it, please blame Ivan Held. Ivan is president of G. P. Putnam's Sons and a lovely man. He and my editor and dear friend Sally Kim suggested it. I was hesitant at first, but then they said they would give me money and I immediately saw what a good idea it was. So I would like to thank them.

Also, a large thanks to Susan Morrison of *The New Yorker*. Susan was kind enough to publish a piece I wrote a few years ago, "Valentine's Day Poems for Married People," which I am told is the most read, most loved, most emailed, and most talked-about piece in the history of *The New Yorker* magazine (although I have no proof of that and I may be thinking of something else).

I would also like to thank the good people at Putnam and Penguin who provided ideas for poems, too many to list here.

I would like to thank a few people I do not know. Real poets. Marie Howe, Mary Oliver, John O'Donoghue, David

Whyte, Seamus Heaney, and Billy Collins. (I can't recommend their work enough. Check out the Poetry Foundation. It's a wonderful site and a deep well of poems and writing about poets.)

My thanks to friends who were kind enough to read and comment on early drafts. Louise Dougherty, Becky and Brian Gray, Debbie Kasher, Lea Mastroberti, Tim LeGallo, Michael Beatty, Dylan Mizner, Nicole Sands, and my brother, Tim Kenney, whose comment, "I thought these were supposed to be funny," was helpful editorial direction.

A huge thanks to my mother-in-law and pal, Linda Funke, for reading, editing, and making all of this better.

And my wife, Lissa. When I wrote the piece in *The New Yorker*, a neighbor of ours stopped my wife and said, "I'm so sorry John wrote all those poems about you. And also about your baggy underpants." The piece wasn't about her or us. They were made up. I count myself exceptionally lucky to be married to a woman who is my best friend and who I text most days to say, *I can't wait for our evening*.

Lissa, if you are reading this, I am fond of you and we should make out soon, if that is something that would be of interest to you. If not, I totally understand.

ABOUT THE AUTHOR

John Kenney is the author of *Talk to Me* and *Truth in Advertising*, which won the Thurber Prize for American Humor. He has worked for many years as a copywriter. Kenney has also been a contributor to *The New Yorker* magazine since 1999. He lives in Brooklyn, New York.